# COLORFUL
# *Curly Haired*
# CRAFTS FOR KIDS

**60** Fun and Easy Activities that Celebrate
the Beauty of Natural Hair

**CHERYL GAVRIELIDES** Founder of *Creative Mama Che*

PAGE STREET
PUBLISHING CO.

PAGE STREET
PUBLISHING CO.

First published in 2022 by

Page Street Publishing Co.

27 Congress Street, Suite 1511

Salem, MA 01970

www.pagestreetpublishing.com

Distributed by Macmillan, sales in Canada by The Canadian Manda Group.

26   25   24   23   22      1   2   3   4   5

ISBN-13: 978-1-64567-474-0

ISBN-10: 1-64567-474-6

Library of Congress Control Number: 2021944913

Cover and book design by Kylie Alexander for Page Street Publishing Co.

Photography by Cheryl Gavrielides

Printed and bound in the United States of America

## DEDICATION

This book is dedicated to my babies,
Andreas and Savannah. I hope we can craft and
create for many more years to come!

# TABLE OF Contents

# INTRODUCTION

Hey there crafters,

I am so glad you are here to join in the curly, crafty fun!

I'm Cheryl—some know me as "Creative Mama Che." I am mama to two curly beauties. We love to craft and have fun. I cannot wait to share our cool, curly crafts with you!

Now, this is no ordinary craft book. You will be exploring a range of fun textures, methods and materials while expressing your own creativity. And most importantly, these crafts celebrate the beauty of natural curly hair!

This collection of 60 projects is a labor of love that I hope will inspire you! I want you to enjoy the process of crafting and creating without worrying about the final product. Everyone's art looks a little different and that is okay. In fact, I want you to be inventive and make things that are as unique as you are! If you don't fancy using a paintbrush, why not use an old toothbrush? And if you don't have paints, you can make your own with cornstarch, a couple drops of water and food coloring. The more creative and imaginative you are, the better!

Flip through the book and see what catches your eye. You will find a range of simple, colorful projects that use everyday materials for a fun crafting experience! Some projects will come together quickly, and others may take a little more time. Most of them you will be able to do on your own, while others are fun to do with a friend. You may need to call on a grown-up to help you with some of the crafts, too!

You might not have thought of it this way, but natural curly hair comes in such a range of textures, styles and colors—just like ART! I hope that my curly crafts will encourage you to see curly hair as unique and beautiful.

When you embark on the different projects, think about all the amazing differences in culture, skin tones, facial features and hair textures of the people around you. Have fun celebrating our differences!

Happy crafting!

Cheryl

# RECYCLE AND REUSE

It brings me so much joy to turn our recycled waste into something new. It just takes a little imagination!

I use mostly recycled materials from around the house. There's so much that can be used for play and crafts! In fact, I have a giant box of recycled bits and bobs ready for crafting. There are cardboard boxes, bottle caps, pieces of bubble wrap, egg cartons, cereal boxes, toilet paper rolls and paper towel rolls.

Perhaps you could start your own collection too.

Recycling and reusing are earth friendly and don't cost a penny!

## CARDBOARD!

As you flip through this book, you'll see that I especially love to use recycled cardboard as the basis for my crafts. You could say I am a bit of a cardboard hoarder!

### A LITTLE TRICK . . .

If you want to store up a good supply of cardboard, whenever you receive a cardboard box, instead of storing the box in one big piece, cut the box up along its folded edges into squares or rectangles. Then you will have your own stash of smaller pieces ready to use the next time you want to craft.

However, with most of our curly crafts, you can most certainly use paper or thin cardboard from a recycled cereal box instead. Anything you already have will work!

Once you have your cardboard, paper and materials, you are ready to craft!

# SENSORY MATERIALS

Crafting with materials stored in my kitchen pantry, or from my local bulk food store, is definitely a favorite of mine! Dried beans, dried chickpeas, dried rice, dried pasta and other nonperishable foods in your kitchen cupboard are amazing for sensory play and perfect for crafts. Plus, they are super cheap!

You can turn these ordinary dried foods into fun, colorful play resources.

# RECIPES AND HOW-TOS

In this section you will find a range of recipes and methods needed for some of the crafts in the book. For example, there is a basic play dough recipe with alternative flavors, a sensory tray and wipeable boards tutorial and more. Some recipes might involve cooking or some trickier techniques, so please ask a grown-up for help! Remember to take a look at the method before you begin the craft, as some recipes might call for the materials to dry overnight!

# POPCORN

**Who doesn't love popcorn? It is super simple to make your own using only popcorn kernels and a little oil. Don't forget to get a grown-up to help you safely use the stove.**

### Materials Needed

Medium pan with a lid

2 tbsp (30 ml) oil

½ cup (96 g) popcorn kernels

### LET'S CRAFT!

Heat the pan over medium-high heat. Add the oil to the pan. Put three popcorn kernels in the pan and put the lid on.

Once you hear the kernels pop, add the remainder of the kernels to the pan and put the lid back on.

Shake the pan a little every minute or so to prevent the kernels from burning. Wait and listen for when the popcorn begins to pop. Stop moving the pan once the popping starts. Take the pan off the heat when you notice the sound of the kernels popping slowing down.

The whole popping process should only take 3 to 4 minutes.

# PLAY DOUGH

We absolutely love play dough, and we love making it too! You probably already have all the ingredients in your cupboards. It's simple to make and so affordable. And of course, there are so many benefits to playing with play dough! Get a grown-up to help you with the hot water.

## Materials Needed

Bowl

2 cups (250 g) flour

½ cup (146 g) salt

2 tbsp (18 g) cream of tartar

3 tbsp (45 ml) vegetable oil

Food coloring

1–1½ cups (240–360 ml) boiling water

Spoon

Scented add-ins: spices, cocoa powder, etc. (optional)

## LET'S CRAFT!

In a bowl, mix the flour, salt and cream of tartar together, then add the oil. Add a few drops of food coloring to the boiling water and stir. Add the colored hot water to the bowl.

Mix it all together with a spoon. Once slightly cooled, mix and knead with your hands. Keep kneading until you have perfect play dough!

Repeat the steps for different colors.

Wrap the dough in plastic wrap and store it in an airtight container. It will keep for weeks!

## MIXED-SPICE PLAY DOUGH

Using the same recipe, add 2 tablespoons (8 g) of mixed spice or pumpkin spice, 2 tablespoons (8 g) of cinnamon and 2 teaspoons (5 g) of ground nutmeg to the hot water before you begin to stir. You could also add a drop of brown and orange food coloring.

Add the spiced hot water to the dry ingredients in the bowl.

Mix it all together with a spoon and, once slightly cooled, mix and knead with your hands. Keep kneading until you have perfect play dough!

## CHOCOLATE PLAY DOUGH

To turn the play dough recipe into a delicious-smelling chocolate dough, just reduce the flour to 1½ cups (188 g) and add ½ cup (43 g) of cocoa powder. The rest of the recipe remains the same!

# CARDBOARD SENSORY BASE

Creating your own cardboard sensory base makes sensory play more engaging and exciting. The best thing about it is that you can create a play base tailored to your very own interests!

You will need to use a glue gun for these bases, so ask a grown-up to help you.

## Materials Needed

2 pieces of cardboard

Pencil

Shape or object to trace

Markers or crayons (optional)

Glue gun

Scissors

## LET'S CRAFT!

On a piece of cardboard, draw the outline of the shape or object that you want to turn into a sensory base. Make it as simple as possible. If you want to add color with markers or crayons, it's best to do it before you add the edges.

Have an adult turn on the glue gun.

Cut the second cardboard piece into thin ½-inch (1.3-cm) strips.

Now you are ready to add the strips to the edges of your picture. Reference image on page 56 for strip placement.

Ask a grown up to apply hot glue along the outline you have drawn. Start off with just a short section to begin with, and then press one of the cardboard strips onto the glue and hold it in place for a few seconds. Continue adding a bit more glue along the outline and pressing the cardboard strips down firmly. You might need to trim some of the strips, so have your scissors handy. Repeat this process until you have created a complete border with the cardboard strips in the shape you have drawn. It takes a little practice, but once you give it a go, it will all make sense!

## CREATIVE TIP

*When you start a new strip, add a little blob of hot glue on the end of the previous strip and stick them together to prevent gaps.*

# COLORED SENSORY FILLERS

I love all sensory play materials, but colored rice, chickpeas and breakfast cereal are especially perfect for pouring and scooping up. You can make a range of colors to fill a cardboard sensory base, and they make great fillers for a range of different sensory trays. You will likely have all the ingredients already at home, and it is so simple and fun to make!

## Materials Needed

1 cup (185 g) uncooked rice, couscous, popcorn kernels, white beans, chickpeas or breakfast cereal

Resealable plastic bag

Food coloring

Vinegar or hand sanitizer

Paint (optional)

Baking sheet

Parchment paper

## LET'S CRAFT!

Add the rice to the resealable bag. You can also use couscous, popcorn kernels or white beans instead of rice. Add a couple drops of food coloring and a drop of vinegar or hand sanitizer.

Seal the bag and remove any air. Shake and mix!

Ensure all the rice is fully coated and the color is well distributed.

Line a baking sheet with parchment paper. Pour the rice out onto the tray.

Leave it to dry overnight. Once dry, mix the rice to ensure it is all separated and ready to play with.

Store it in an airtight container or a clean resealable bag and it will keep well for months!

## COLORED CHICKPEAS

Use the same recipe to make colored chickpeas, except replace the food coloring and vinegar with a few squirts of paint.

## COLORED BREAKFAST CEREAL

Use the same recipe to make colored breakfast cereal, except replace the vinegar with 1 tablespoon (15 ml) of water.

# HOMEMADE CLAY

**We love using clay to make keepsakes and play accessories! This recipe is easy and fun to mold and play with. When your creations dry, you can keep them for years! Be sure to get a grown-up's help using the stove and oven.**

## Materials Needed

Saucepan

2 cups (230 g) baking soda

1 cup (120 g) cornstarch

1½ cups (355 ml) water

Spoon

Glass or heat-proof container

Baking sheet

Parchment paper

## LET'S CRAFT!

In a pan over medium heat, combine the baking soda, cornstarch and water. Stir the mixture until the consistency resembles mashed potatoes.

Remove the pan from the heat and transfer the mixture to a glass or heat-proof container. Leave it to cool.

Preheat the oven to 320°F (160°C). Line a baking sheet with parchment paper.

Once the clay is cool and you can knead it with your hands, you are ready to create your clay shapes!

Turn the oven off and add your clay models to the prepared baking sheet. Bake the models in the warmed oven for about 30 minutes, then remove the tray from the oven.

Turn the oven on again. After 5 minutes, turn it off. Flip your clay models over and put them in the warm oven again for another 30 minutes.

Remove the tray from the oven, take the models off the tray and let them dry overnight. The next day, they should be hard and ready to play with!

# WIPEABLE BOARDS

It is so easy to make a board that you can draw and paint on and then wipe it clean, ready to create new art over and over again.

Follow these instructions to make your own wipeable boards!

## Materials Needed

Black marker

Thin cardboard

Self-adhesive film (adhesive tape will work as an alternative)

Scissors

## LET'S CRAFT!

Draw a picture on the thin cardboard.

Unroll the self-adhesive film and lay it across the thin cardboard to measure how much you need.

Cut the self-adhesive film so it overlaps the piece of card on each side by approximately ¾ inch (2 cm).

Unpeel about 1½ inches (3 cm) from the film backing on one side and stick it to the left side of the thin cardboard, leaving some excess film that will overhang. Continue to pull the paper to release the self-adhesive film while using your hands to stick it firmly onto the thin cardboard. At the same time, try to smooth out and remove any air bubbles.

Ensure the entire side is covered.

Fold the overhanging self-adhesive film around the back so that it is tightly covering the thin cardboard. This is your wipeable board!

*See image on page 83.

# FIZZING POWDER

**To create your own fizzing fun, all you need is a few ingredients!**

## Materials Needed

Cup or jug

Dish soap

¼ cup (60 ml) water

Small bowl

¼ cup (55 g) baking soda

Food coloring

Spoon

Baking sheet

Parchment paper

White vinegar or apple cider vinegar

## LET'S CRAFT!

In a cup or jug, gently mix a couple drops of dish soap with the water. Try not to make it foam and bubble! Set it aside.

In a small bowl, combine the baking soda and a couple drops of food coloring. If making more than one color of fizzing powder, repeat this step with ¼ cup (55 g) of baking soda for each color.

Add the soapy water, 1 tablespoon (15 ml) at a time, to each bowl of baking soda and mix until it forms a stiff paste. It should not be too wet!

Line a baking sheet with parchment paper. Scoop each paste mixture onto the lined baking sheet and leave it to dry overnight. Once dry, crumble the large clumps with your fingers into a powder.

When you are ready to play, drop or pour some vinegar on the powder and watch it bubble and fizz!

# Colorful
# CURLY CREATIONS

Don't bright colors just make you smile? Well, this chapter is full of fun craft ideas that are exciting and bursting with color!

Using simple methods and only a few supplies and materials, these projects will brighten up your day. You will use a range of new, exciting techniques to paint and explore a range of textures from Finger Paint 'Fro (page 33) to Bubble Wrap Curls (page 34). Create your own wipeable boards for lots of styling fun (page 25), and try painting on packing peanuts (page 21).

I can'l wait for you to create some amazing colorful art!

# DISCO 'FRO

Do you like creating colorful patterns? This brightly colored chickpea art is a lot of fun to make, and once you have prepared the colored chickpeas (see page 12), you can use them for a variety of other crafts and sensory play!

I love these neon colors, but you can use any of your favorite colors.

## Materials Needed

Thin cardboard

Black marker and/or colored pens

1 batch colored chickpeas in neon colors (page 12)

Plate or bowl

Craft glue

## LET'S CRAFT!

Draw a woman's face in profile with an afro on a piece of thin cardboard using the black marker and/or colored pens.

Put your colored chickpeas on a plate or in a bowl.

Now it is time to decorate the afro with the colorful chickpeas. Use the glue to stick them on. Can you create a rainbow or colorful shapes within the afro?

# PACKING PEANUT PLAITS

Have you ever received a package in the mail before that contained packing peanuts? Instead of throwing them out, you can reuse them in this craft. The amazing part is what happens when you paint on them!

## Materials Needed

Cardboard

Black marker

Glue stick

Packing peanuts

Paint (I used a metallic paint, but any colors would work well)

Paintbrush

Water

## LET'S CRAFT!

Draw a face with a plaits hairstyle on a piece of cardboard with the black marker. It can be a very simple picture.

Now glue the packing peanuts to the plaits. Once the glue has dried, it is time to paint!

You can use whatever colors you would like. Make sure to wash the paintbrush in water when you want to use a new color. What happens when you paint on the packing peanuts? They start to melt! Don't you love the way it looks? I bet your picture looks great!

## LET'S TALK

*This is a great opportunity to think about change and textures and how hair can change with washing, different weather conditions, humidity, etc.!*

# YOGURT PAINTING

**Did you know you can paint with yogurt? That's right— the very yogurt you eat can be fun to paint with too. The texture of it is amazing! We will be making a wipeable board so you can create fun pictures over and over again.**

## Materials Needed

Thin cardboard

Black marker and/or colored pens

Scissors

Self-adhesive film

½ cup (123 g) plain yogurt

¼ cup (30 g) cornstarch

4 bowls

Food coloring in 4 different colors

Spoon

Paintbrushes

## LET'S CRAFT!

Draw a face with a large afro on a piece of thin cardboard using the black marker and/or colored pens. Make the afro as big as you can.

Using the scissors, follow the instructions on page 14 to cover the thin cardboard with self-adhesive film to make it a wipeable board.

To make your yogurt paints, combine 2 tablespoons (31 g) of yogurt and 1 heaping tablespoon (8 g) of cornstarch in each bowl. Add a couple drops of food coloring to each bowl, each in a different color, and mix with a spoon.

These are your yogurt paints!

Now it is time to get creative. You aren't limited to just painting the hair—you could also have a go at painting the face you drew too. Happy painting!

## EXTEND YOUR PLAY

*Why not add the colored yogurt to a shallow tray and have fun drawing pictures with your fingers? You could also practice writing letters and numbers.*

# WIPEABLE STYLES

What is your favorite hairstyle? Chop and change hairstyles with this wipeable face board. The reason we love these boards is that you get to create styles and faces over and over again. Just wipe and start over!

## Materials Needed

Black marker and/or colored pens

Thin cardboard

Scissors

Self-adhesive film

Whiteboard pens or chalk pens

Tissue/whiteboard eraser

## LET'S CRAFT!

With the black marker and/or colored pens, draw a circle shape for a face on the bottom half of your piece of thin cardboard, leaving space for hairstyles on the top half. Using the scissors, follow the instructions on page 14 to cover the thin cardboard with self-adhesive film to make it a wipeable board.

Now it is time to create fun styles and faces! Using the board pens, can you draw a happy face, sad face or a silly face? What kind of hairstyles can you draw? How about using rainbow colors, or groups of colors that remind you of your favorite candies or ice cream! You could even use many different shades of just one of your favorite colors! Once you have created each face, you can create a new one. Just wipe it away with a tissue and start again!

## CURLY TIP

*Talk about different styles and hair textures. For example, what is your favorite protective style? Do you like cornrows, twists or locs? Perhaps you could draw a style that you love but haven't worn yet!*

# UNCLE'S LOCS

Sometimes we can use scientific processes, such as "absorption," to create art! Have you ever tried raised salt painting? Using simple materials like salt and glue, you can create fun and amazing scientific art.

**Are you ready to be amazed?**

## Materials Needed

Thin cardboard

Pencil

Black marker

Rimmed baking sheet

Craft glue with a fine-tip applicator

Table salt in a cup or small jug

Paint

Water

Paint palette

Paintbrushes

## LET'S CRAFT!

Draw a face with dreadlocks on a piece of thin cardboard using the pencil and black marker.

Place your picture on the rimmed baking sheet. This will keep all the messiness in one place.

Apply a line of glue along the middle of each dreadlock.

Sprinkle the salt onto the glue until the glue is completely covered.

Pick up your picture and carefully let all the excess salt fall back into the baking sheet. You can reuse this salt for other activities or to make play dough!

Let it dry for a few hours, or overnight.

Once dry, mix a couple drops of paint with 1 to 2 tablespoons (15 to 30 ml) of water on the paint palette. Dip a paintbrush into the watery paint.

Touch the brush gently to the salt. Can you see the colored water travel up the salt? How amazing!

Continue this process until you have created a colorful salt art picture.

## CREATIVE TIP

*As an alternative, you can use food coloring and water instead of paint. Just mix until you have colored water, and use the same technique with the paintbrush.*

# CURLY BUILDING BRICK PRINTS

Do you enjoy creating with building bricks? We certainly do! But have you ever tried painting with your bricks? It is so much fun and creates the most amazing spot patterns that are perfect for making curl art.

## Materials Needed

Cardboard or recycled cereal box

Black marker and/or colored pens

Paints

Paint palette

Building bricks

Paintbrush

## LET'S CRAFT!

Draw a face with a curly 'fro on a piece of cardboard using the black marker and/or colored pens. Prepare your paints on the paint palette and building bricks for painting.

See if you can guess how many "spots" it will take to fill the afro before you begin.

Using a paintbrush, brush some of the first color you wish to use onto a building brick. Now firmly press the building brick into the 'fro area of the cardboard. Repeat to make prints in the hair section. You can overlap the circles too and make as many prints as you like!

What kind of patterns can you make?

## GET CREATIVE

*Why not try using both small and large building blocks to make cool prints?*

# BUN FULL OF BUTTONS

**Buttons for crafts? Yes! They're not only for your clothes—you can also make amazing art with them. And because they come in so many different shapes, colors and sizes, they are awesome to craft with.**

## Materials Needed

Cardboard

Black marker and/or colored pens

Buttons of different colors and sizes

2 bowls

Craft glue

Paintbrush

## LET'S CRAFT!

Draw a face with hair in a top bun on a piece of cardboard using the black marker and/or colored pens.

Place the buttons in a bowl; it makes it a lot easier to craft with them.

Pour some craft glue into a second bowl.

Use a paintbrush to apply the glue and stick the buttons to the bun! You can create patterns or just enjoy the process and use a mix of colors and sizes like I did.

What do you think? I love it!

# FINGER PAINT 'FRO

I love messy crafts! Do you?

Who needs a paintbrush when we can use our very own fingers? That's right—get ready to get a little messy while creating a curly piece of art.

## Materials Needed

Thin cardboard

Black marker and/or colored pens

Paint in 5 different colors

Paint palette or plate

## LET'S CRAFT!

Draw a face with an afro on a piece of thin cardboard using the black marker and/or colored pens. You can color in the face if you want to.

Squeeze out a little of each paint color onto a palette or plate.

Choose which color to use first, dip one finger in it and press that finger onto the afro you drew. Repeat with all the colors until you have a multicolored 'fro.

Check out your colorful art and colorful fingers!

# BUBBLE WRAP CURLS

It's always fun to paint on new textures and surfaces! The bubble wrap creates the most amazing curly art, and the bubbles feel so different when you paint on them. The next time you receive some bubble wrap in the mail, you have to try this out!

## Materials Needed

Black marker

Cardboard or a recycled cereal box

Scissors

Bubble wrap

Pen

Tape

Paintbrushes

Paints in a variety of colors

## LET'S CRAFT!

With a black marker, draw a face with a large curly afro on a piece of cardboard. Cut around the outline with scissors. You may need a grown-up to help you.

Now place the bubble wrap on top of the afro section. With a pen, trace the outline of the bottom part of the hair on the bubble wrap and cut along that line. Apply a small piece of tape to keep the bubble wrap in place. Then cut around the afro, leaving a border of approximately 1½ inches (3 cm).

Prepare a few pieces of tape that are ready to use, and fold the extra bubble wrap behind the cardboard so it fits tightly around the afro, securing it with the tape. You should have a nice bubble wrap afro. Now it is time to paint!

Using paintbrushes, decorate your bubble wrap afro with a range of colorful paints. How does it feel to paint on bubble wrap?

Doesn't your bubble wrap curly art look amazing?

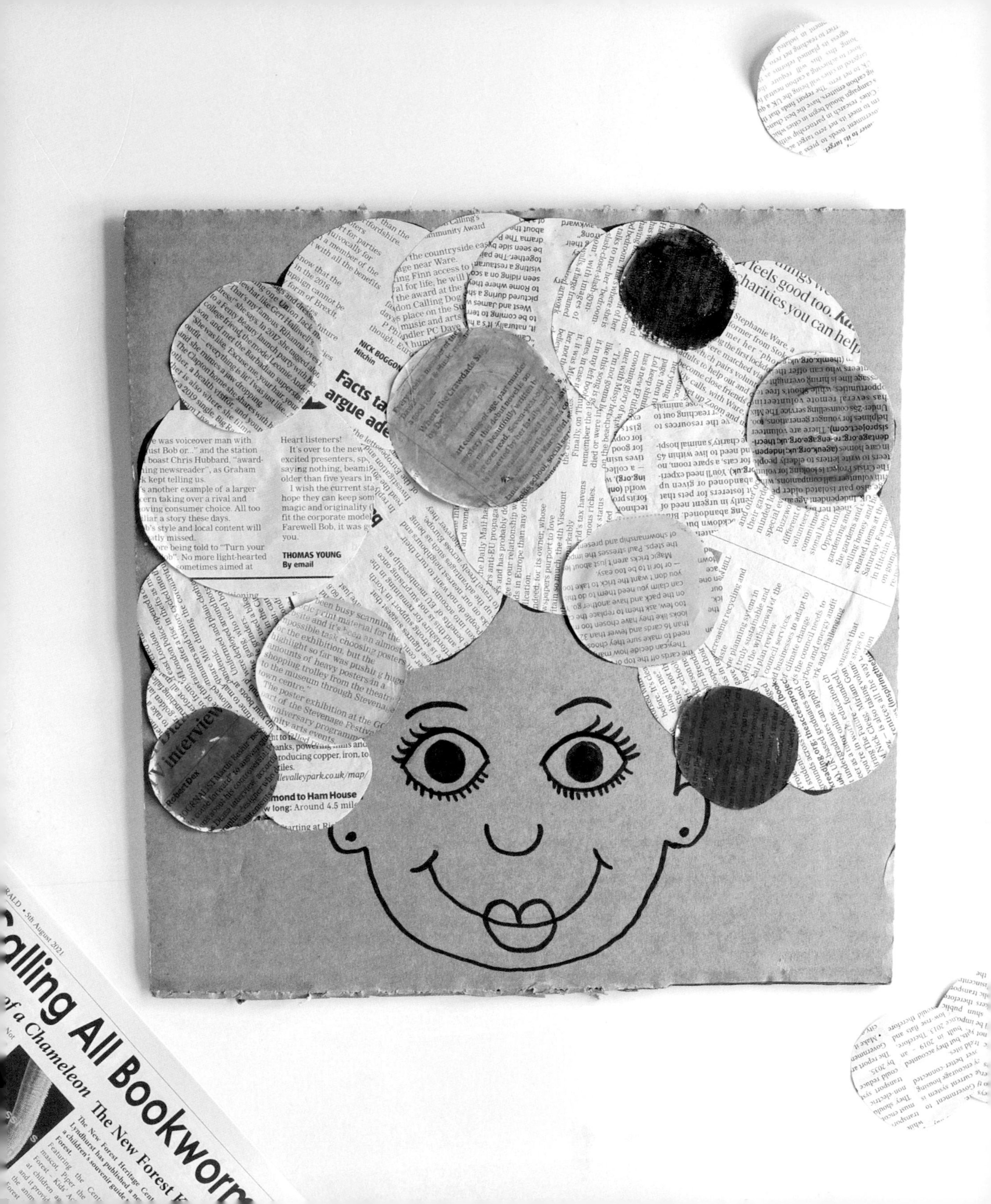

THOMAS YOUNG
By email
The New Forest
of a Chameleon

# MAGAZINE MANE

**Have you ever made a magazine collage before? This cool piece of art is so simple to make with paper clippings and glue. Old magazines, books and newspapers all make great collage materials.**

**Are you ready to make a magazine mane?**

## Materials Needed

Black marker

Thin cardboard

Scissors

Magazine, old book or newspaper

Paint pens or felt-tip markers

Glue stick

## LET'S CRAFT!

With a black marker, draw a face with an afro on a piece of thin cardboard. Cut out a range of different-sized circles from your magazine, book or newspaper with your scissors.

Use paint pens or felt-tip markers to color in 8 to 10 of the circles.

Arrange all the circles inside the border of the afro to ensure you have enough to cover the entire hair section.

Stick them in place with a glue stick. How cool does that look? I love how complementary the printed circles look with a few pops of color!

# MIX AND MATCH CLAY FACE

We love to make clay models and enjoy painting them afterward too! Have you ever made your own clay? It is very easy to make, but you will need a grown-up to help you.

## Materials Needed

1 batch Homemade Clay (page 13)

Rolling pin

Parchment paper

Cereal bowl

Butter knife

Baking sheet

Paints

Paintbrushes

Black marker

## LET'S CRAFT!

Once your clay is ready to mold, use a rolling pin to roll it out in an even layer on a piece of parchment paper. Using the bowl as a guide, cut out one circle with the butter knife and set it aside on a baking sheet lined with parchment paper. To create the hair, use the bowl again to cut out two larger semicircles that will fit on the top part of the face.

Now use the butter knife and your fingers to create two afro shapes from the semicircles.

When you have finished, ask an adult to help you follow the instructions on page 13 to dry the clay.

Paint the face using skin tone paint. You can mix your own shades just like I did! Paint the hair in a range of colors or use multiple colors for rainbow hair. Let the paint dry then add a facial expression and curl patterns using a black marker.

Mix and match the afros to the face and have fun with your new clay models!

## CREATIVE TIP

*Use any extra clay to create the features and expressions of your face for a more 3D look.*

# WASH GLOVE HAIR LOVE

Do you enjoy finger painting? If you do, then you will enjoy this fun twist on finger painting that incorporates a washcloth glove. You might have an old one around the house, or you can get them super cheap at your local dollar store.

## Materials Needed

Cardboard or recycled cereal box

Black marker and/or colored pens

Washable paints

Paint palette or plate

Washcloth glove

## LET'S CRAFT!

Draw a face and an outline of your favorite hairstyle on a piece of cardboard using a black marker and/or colored pens.

Add some of each color of washable paint to your paint palette or a plate.

Put the washcloth glove on one hand; you will be using each finger for a different color. How would you describe the texture of these fingerprints? Dab paint on the afro until you have a colorful 'fro!

What do you think?

## CREATIVE TIP

*If you don't have a washcloth glove, you can use an old winter glove.*

# INVITATION TO COLOR

**Do you enjoy coloring pictures? I certainly do! Coloring is a great way to express yourself, and it is also very relaxing. You can be as creative as you wish and use your favorite markers, crayons, pens or paint!**

## Materials Needed

Cardboard or a recycled cereal box

Pencil

Your favorite pens, markers or paint

## LET'S CRAFT!

Draw a scene of your friends on a piece of cardboard with a pencil.

Now spend time relaxing and coloring it in. Maybe you could do this with your friends and talk about your favorite hairstyles, foods or kinds of clothes.

Whatever art supplies you have decided to use, just have fun with this activity. Why not color the hair in your favorite colors? Be as creative as you want!

# SUNCATCHER AFRO

**Have you ever made a suncatcher? They look so pretty in the sun as they reflect beautiful colors onto the floor and walls!**

## Materials Needed

Thin cardboard

Black marker

Scissors

Cellophane in different colors

Glue stick

## LET'S CRAFT!

Draw a face with an afro on a piece of thin cardboard with a black marker. Make the afro as simple as possible because you will be cutting it out.

Lightly fold the thin cardboard in the middle of the afro. Using scissors, begin to cut out the entire section of hair, leaving a border of about 1 inch (2.5 cm). Ask an adult for help if you need it.

Next, cut pieces of cellophane in different colors to fit slightly over the cut-out area. Now turn the drawing over and glue the cellophane pieces to the thin cardboard and to each other using the glue stick.

Ensure the entire afro is covered with the colorful cellophane.

Once it is dry, it is time to go outside and let the sunlight shine through it! How beautiful does it look when the colors reflect on the walls and the ground?

## CREATIVE TIP

*If you cannot find cellophane at your local craft store or online, you can use cellophane from caramel and hard candy wrappers.*

# "JUST LIKE ME" BAG

Have you ever considered designing your own bag before? It is definitely possible!

The beauty of cardboard crafts is that you can make pretty much anything you want. So, are you ready to create a custom bag that looks like you?

## Materials Needed

Black marker

2 large pieces of cardboard or recycled cereal boxes

Felt-tip pens

Scissors

Ruler

Pencil

Glue gun

27½-inch (70-cm)-thick cotton cord or jute rope

## NEED HELP?

*If the cardboard you are using is very thick, a craft knife might be necessary to cut it out. This is a tool that only a grown-up should handle! Don't be afraid to ask for help as you make this bag.*

## LET'S CRAFT!

With the black marker, draw three large circles on a piece of cardboard, each approximately 6 inches (15 cm) in diameter.

On one of the circles, draw a picture of your face. Add hair and color it in with felt-tip pens. It can be as colorful as you like! Cut the face and hair out and set it aside.

Cut out the other two circles. Using a ruler, measure 2 inches (5 cm) from the top center of each one, draw a horizontal line with the pencil and cut off the top sections.

On another piece of cardboard, measure and draw a rectangle that is approximately 13 x 3 inches (33 x 8 cm), then cut it out. This will be the base of your bag.

The next part involves using the hot glue gun, so ask a grown-up to help you. Start with one of the circles with the top section cut off. Use the glue gun to glue it to the rectangle strip so that the edges and corners line up. Repeat this process with the other circle so that you have formed a "pouch."

Now glue the cotton cord onto one of the circles to make handles that will go over your shoulder.

Last, glue your face to the side of the pouch with the string so that the string is covered.

And there you have it! What do you think of your new bag? How cute does it look?

Why not make one for a friend? They make great homemade gifts!

# Diverse Play
## WITH SENSORY TRAYS

If you love to explore, discover, create, mix, scoop and pour, then you will love this chapter!

Sensory play encourages you to use your imagination and creativity. It can even inspire you to create your own games and competitions, as with Beans and Beards (page 50); practice counting, as with Chocolate Cereal People (page 58); and discuss a range of topics, invent characters and explore and discuss textures, as with the Rainbow Hair Play Tray (page 57).

As you explore these trays, talk to your friends and family, discuss your ideas and have fun!

Sensory trays do not have to be complicated. Check out the Bottle Cap 'Fro (page 53), for example. All you need is recycled bottle caps for lots of fun and play!

Go on, get started! I can't wait for you to explore, imagine and have fun!

# BEANS AND BEARDS

Did you know you can play and make crafts with dried foods? Dried beans are great for making instruments, sticking on crafts, counting and more. But my little ones love when they're added to a tray so they can play with them freely. Pouring, scooping and filling up a range of bowls and containers can add up to hours of fun. Let's create a fun base so that you can enjoy this sensory play, too!

## Materials Needed

Cardboard

Black marker and/or colored pens

Cardboard strips

Scissors

Glue gun

Craft glue

Large plastic tray or container

Dried beans (any variety)

Bowls

Scooping and grabbing utensils (bowls, scoops, tongs)

## LET'S CRAFT!

Draw a man with an afro and beard on a piece of cardboard with the black marker and/or colored pens. With an adult's help, follow the instructions on page 11 to turn the man into a sensory base with the cardboard strips, scissors and glue gun. This will allow you to fill his hair and beard with beans. Add the sensory base to the tray.

Add the beans to a bowl and place it on the tray. Also include a range of bowls, scoops and tongs for added fun.

Now explore the tray! Can you fill the hair and beard with beans? Can you create an interesting pattern for the hair?

## EXTEND YOUR PLAY

*How about a game? Who can scoop the most beans into a bowl with a spoon in 20 seconds? Who can pick up the most beans with tongs in 30 seconds? What other games can you come up with?*

# BOTTLE CAP 'FRO

Have you ever thought about saving bottle caps for craft activities? Well, get collecting! You could even ask your friends and family to save them for you. This sensory tray is so much fun that you will be making up games for hours!

## Materials Needed

Cardboard

Black marker and/or colored pens

Recycled bottle caps

Glue gun

Large plastic tray or container

Pom-poms or felt balls

Scooping and grabbing utensils (scoops, bowls, tongs)

## LET'S CRAFT!

Draw a face with an afro on a piece of cardboard using the black marker and/or colored pens.

Flip the bottle caps upside down and arrange them on the afro. Don't worry if there are gaps! When you are happy with the placement, ask an adult to help you glue them to the cardboard with the glue gun.

Place the face in the center of your tray. Add the pom-poms to the tray along with a range of sensory resources such as tongs, bowls and scoops.

Now have fun! Can you match the pom-poms to the colors of the bottle caps? Can you bounce the pom-poms so that they land in the bottle caps?

Play a game where you take turns to see how quickly you can use the tongs to pick up pom-poms and place them in all the bottle caps. How many seconds did it take?

Explore the tray and see what other games you can invent!

# HAIR WRAP SENSORY BAG

**Sensory bags are great mess-free sensory play. They are easy to make and fun to play with! And who doesn't love a super squishy pouch to play with!**

## Materials Needed

Cardboard

Pencil

Black marker/Colored pens

A tablespoon

Clear hair gel

Water

Ziplock bag

Approximately 20 pom-poms in 4 or 5 colors

Adhesive tape

## LET'S CRAFT!

On a piece of cardboard, use a pencil to draw a person wearing a head wrap. Trace the pencil drawing with black marker. Choose four or five colored pens to match your pom-poms and make sure to color the parts of your head wrap in separate sections as seen in the picture. Put this aside while we make the sensory bag.

Mix 4 tablespoons of clear hair gel with 4 tablespoons (60 ml) of water. Mix the water and gel together and add the pom-poms to the bag. Remove all air bubbles and seal the bag. Seal the top of the bag completely with tape.

Now grab your drawing and tape it to the table or floor.

Put your sensory bag on top of your drawing and tape it on all four sides.

Now it's time to color with pom-poms! Use the edge of your finger to push all the pom-poms onto the correct colors.

Don't forget to squish it too!

# RAINBOW HAIR PLAY TRAY

Do you love hair accessories such as beads and cuffs?

**This tray combines colored rice with beads and other hair accessories for fun exploration and play. Not only will you enjoy creating this tray, but you will also enjoy the sensory experience while making up fun games!**

**Make the rainbow rice in advance so you will be ready to play!**

## Materials Needed

Cardboard or recycled cereal box

Black marker and/or colored pens

Cardboard strips

Scissors

Glue gun

Large rimmed tray or baking sheet

5 batches colored rice in different colors (page 12)

5 bowls

Hair accessories (beads, cuffs, clips, etc.)

Scooping and pouring utensils (scoops, spoons, bowls)

## LET'S CRAFT!

Draw a face with a large afro on a piece of cardboard using the black marker and/or colored pens. With an adult's help, follow the instructions on page 11 to turn the afro into a sensory base with the cardboard strips, scissors and glue gun. Add the sensory base to the tray.

Add your colored rice to five separate bowls.

Can you create a rainbow 'fro and decorate it with the hair accessories?

Scoop, mix, pour and explore. Have a go at making fun patterns and pictures using your fingers in the rice!

# CHOCOLATE CEREAL PEOPLE

We call this project a "snack-tivity" because it involves playing with breakfast cereal! That's right—this is an activity where you can use all your senses, including taste. But do not eat the cereal all at once; you want some left to explore and play with.

## Materials Needed

Scissors

2 paper towel roll tubes

Colored pens and pencils

Craft glue

Materials for hair (wool, yarn, felt, cotton)

Chocolate crispy rice cereal or your favorite cereal

Medium rimmed tray or baking sheet

Scooping and pouring utensils (scoops, spoons, bowls)

## LET'S CRAFT!

Using the scissors, cut each paper towel roll into two or three smaller tubes. You might need to ask a grown-up for help.

Decorate the paper towel rolls with faces using colored pens and pencils, then glue on some hair using different materials. Why not try drawing some of your friends or family? Can you create their hair too?

What do you think of your paper towel roll people?

Now it's time to have some fun with them! Add enough cereal to a medium rimmed tray to cover the bottom. Next, add your paper towel roll people and scooping utensils. Explore, scoop, fill and pour!

## EXTEND YOUR PLAY

*Practice counting, addition and subtraction using the cereal and paper towel roll people. Can you guess how many spoonfuls of cereal will fit in each one?*

# GRANDMA'S RICE AND BEANS

**I was inspired by the popular Caribbean "rice and peas" (though the dish actually uses kidney beans), and it just made sense to try out a fun sensory play version! Have fun creating Grandma's afro before having lots of sensory fun!**

## Materials Needed

Cardboard

Pencil

Black marker/colored pens

Scissors or craft knife (ask a grown-up to help with this)

Rimmed tray or serving tray (or a large container will work)

Craft glue

2 cups (380 g) uncooked rice

Paintbrush

Small dollop of paint (any color)

Box/shoebox

1 cup (184 g) dried kidney beans

Bowl

Scoops, spoons and tongs

## EXTEND YOUR PLAY

*Why not add some dice, roll a number and see who can use tongs to pick up the correct number of beans and feed it to Grandma the quickest?*

## LET'S CRAFT!

Draw a picture on cardboard in pencil of one of your grandparents or another family member. Outline the pencil in black marker.

Ask a grown-up to cut it out and cut out the mouth area (as seen in the picture) and place it in the tray you will be using to play with.

Now spread the craft glue on half of the afro and pour the rice onto the glued section. Leave it for about half a minute, then shake off the excess rice. (The excess rice will go straight into the tray ready to play with!) Repeat this process on the other side of the afro so that you have an entire afro covered in rice.

Leave this to dry for a few hours or overnight.

When it is dry, get a paintbrush and gently dab the paint onto the rice. You can use any color you want!

Once the paint is dry, stick Grandma onto the box with glue.

Now ask a grown-up to help you cut the mouth section out on the box.

Pour out the remainder of the rice to completely fill the bottom of the tray. Add the box and Grandma on top. Pour out the beans into a bowl and add the sensory tools around the tray.

Now explore and feed Grandma! I wonder what fun games you can come up with!

# ALL AROUND THE WORLD

Do you have friends from other countries who speak different languages, have different skin tones or have different hair than you? Isn't it amazing that we all look so unique? This DIY Earth tray is a celebration of all different types of people from around the world.

## Materials Needed

Scissors

Cardboard or recycled cereal boxes

Pencil

Black marker

Colored pencils or markers

Paint pens

Cardboard strips

Scissors

Glue gun

Large plastic tray or container

Sticky tack

5 batches colored rice in any colors (page 12)

Pastry brush

Scooping and pouring utensils (scoops, spoons, bowls)

## LET'S CRAFT!

Cut out ten 2 x 2–inch (5 x 5–cm) squares of cardboard.

Draw the faces of your friends and family on each piece of cardboard using a pencil and black marker. Color them in with colored pencils or markers and set them aside.

To create the Earth sensory base, draw a simple Earth and continents on a large piece of cardboard 12 inches (30 cm) or larger in diameter and color it in with paint pens. With an adult's help, follow the instructions on page 11 to turn the Earth into a sensory base with the cardboard strips, scissors and glue gun.

Next, it's time to have a little fun! This might get a little messy, so add the Earth base to a large tray or container to contain the rice.

Add a little sticky tack to the back of each picture of your friends and stick them on the Earth picture. Cover it all with the colored rice and, using a pastry brush or your fingers, try to search for your friends. If you are playing with others, get one person to call out one of the names of your friends and see how long it takes you to find them!

Have fun with the colored rice by scooping and pouring!

# Cut, Curl
# AND STYLE CRAFTS

If you love cutting with scissors or have just started using scissors, then this chapter is just for you!

This chapter is all about fun crafts that require cutting, sticking, styling and decorating. You will basically become a crafty hairdresser or barber! Practice cutting homemade chocolate play dough curls (page 81) and have fun "shaving" Daddy's beard using colored shaving cream (page 73).

These curly hair–inspired crafts resemble the many textures, colors and styles of beautiful natural hair. As you curl, style and cut, have fun and let your creativity shine.

# CURLY MOSAIC

A mosaic is a picture made up of small parts, such as pieces of glass or small tiles. But you can create your very own mosaic art using small pieces of construction paper, fabric and other textured materials. Let's create our own curly mosaic!

## Materials Needed

Cardboard or recycled cereal box

Felt-tip pens

Construction paper, tissue paper, foam sheets, felt, fabric and any other textured material

Scissors

Several bowls

Craft glue

Paintbrush

## LET'S CRAFT!

Draw a face with a curly afro, bantu knots or braids on a piece of cardboard using felt-tip pens.

Begin cutting your colored materials into tiny shapes with the scissors. Make as many triangles, squares, circles, rectangles or other shapes as you like. Add each color to a separate bowl. Separating each color makes it easier to create specific color patterns.

Pour some glue into a bowl and you are ready to create!

Using a paintbrush, spread a little glue on each colored shape and adhere them to the hair section you drew. Can you make patterns with the different colors? Take your time with it and have fun!

# UNCLE'S BEARD TRIM

**Have you ever wanted to be a barber or hairdresser? Do you think you would enjoy cutting hair? Well, this fun craft will let you practice your scissor skills! Do you know anyone who has a beard? If you do, use them as inspiration for this project!**

## Materials Needed

Cardboard or recycled cereal box

Black marker

Pencil

Construction paper

Ruler

Scissors

Glue stick

## LET'S CRAFT!

On a piece of cardboard, use a black marker to draw the face of someone you know who has a beard.

Now, can you draw their beard on a sheet of construction paper? You might need a grown-up to help you with this bit! The beard must fit on the face you have already drawn, just below the mouth or around the mouth. It is also important that the beard be approximately 6 inches (15 cm) or more in length from the bottom of the mouth.

Next, draw lines across the beard with a pencil, as shown in the example picture. The lines can be wavy, straight, curly or zigzagged. Can you draw other kinds of lines that aren't pictured?

You are nearly ready to give him a trim! Cut the beard out along the outline and glue the beard onto the face.

Now you are ready to trim the beard! With your scissors, see if you can carefully cut along the lines you drew, starting at the bottom and working your way up. Keep going until you are happy with his beard trim!

# SATIN BONNET PUZZLE

**Did you know that puzzles can help improve your memory and exercise your brain?**

**In this activity you will make your very own puzzle, and it can be as easy or as difficult as you want!**

## Materials Needed

Cardboard or recycled cereal box

Black marker

Colored pens

Scissors

## LET'S CRAFT!

Draw a picture of someone wearing a satin hair bonnet on the cardboard with a black marker.

Now color in the person and the bonnet with colored pens. Use as many colors as you like. Do you have a bonnet of your own? Can you recreate the patterns?

Now it's time to cut the picture up with scissors and turn it into a puzzle. I like to cut the pieces into triangles and rectangles, but you can try to cut them into the same shapes as a jigsaw puzzle.

Once you have made the puzzle, mix the pieces up. Can you put your puzzle together?

Try making more puzzles as gifts for your family and friends!

### DID YOU KNOW?

*Do you own a satin bonnet? Wearing a satin bonnet at night protects natural hair by minimizing hair breakage and keeping moisture in your natural hair! If you wear a satin bonnet to bed, your curls will thank you!*

# DADDY GETS A SHAVE

**Do you know that shaving cream is so much fun to play with? You can enjoy and explore the shaving cream in this activity even after you have "shaved" Daddy's beard. If you like messy activities, then this is for you!**

## Materials Needed

2 pieces thin cardboard

Black marker and/or colored pens

Scissors

Self-adhesive film

Drinking straw

Adhesive tape

Shaving cream

Bowl

Food coloring

Spoon

## LET'S CRAFT!

Draw a face with a large beard on a piece of thin cardboard with the black marker and/or colored pens. Using the scissors, follow the instructions on page 14 to cover the thin cardboard with self-adhesive film to make it a wipeable board.

On a separate piece of thin cardboard, draw a shaving razor like the one pictured and cut it out. Cut the straw so it is the same length as the width of the razor. Use adhesive tape to attach the straw along the bottom of the razor. The straw will make the razor end stronger and it will help you to remove the shaving cream more successfully. Then cover the entire razor with adhesive tape.

Add a few squirts of white shaving cream to a bowl and add a few drops of food coloring. You can use any colors you like! Once you have mixed in the color, you can apply the shaving cream in the shape of a beard to the face you drew.

And now the fun begins!

Use the "razor" to shave the hair and beard. How easily can you remove the shaving cream? You can use your hands too if you like! Shave the beard as many times as you like.

And just remember, getting messy is all part of the fun!

## EXTEND YOUR PLAY

*You can even practice writing letters and numbers in the shaving cream. Or you can spread the shaving cream out on a tray and make fun pictures with your fingers!*

# CURLY CUT

**Do you enjoy cutting paper? My daughter could cut out shapes for hours! These paper curls will keep you busy cutting and perfecting your scissor skills. And they are fun to make too!**

## Materials Needed

Thin cardboard

Black marker and/or colored pens

8½ x 11–inch (22 x 28–cm) sheet cardstock or paper

Scissors

Craft glue

## LET'S CRAFT!

Draw a face with an outline of curls on a piece of thin cardboard with black marker and/or colored pens.

Using scissors, cut the colored cardstock into fourteen 1-inch (2.5-cm) strips.

To make paper curls, open the scissors as wide as you can. Hold the end of a paper strip against one of the blades and press down gently with your thumb as you slide the length of the paper strip between your finger and the scissors. You might need a grown-up to help you!

The paper strip should spiral. You can loosen the curls as little or as much as you like by pulling on them gently.

Once you have enough curls, glue them onto the hair section of the face you drew.

Now get to cutting the loose ends of the curls! Can you create a curly style? Perhaps you could cut zigzags or wavy lines. Or you could cut the curls short. Have fun cutting and trimming!

# RASHIDA'S BRAIDS

Have you ever had your hair braided? It is my favorite protective hairstyle! Now you can have fun with this bead-threading braid craft. You can also practice braiding in preparation for this activity. Let's get braiding!

## Materials Needed

Thick wool

Thin cardboard

Black marker and/or colored pens

Scissors

Sharp pencil or pen

Adhesive tape

Hair accessories (beads, cuffs, clips, etc.)

## LET'S CRAFT!

Using the wool, create six braids, using three strands of wool for each braid. If you can't braid yet, you can twist the wool or use a single piece of thick wool or have a grown-up help you braid. Once you have made six braids, set them aside.

Draw the side profile of a face with braids on a piece of thin cardboard with the black marker and/or colored pens and cut it out using scissors. Make sure there is enough space to add the braided wool.

Ask a grown-up to pierce six evenly spaced holes with a sharp pencil or pen in the braided area of the profile you cut out.

Feed your braids through the holes and use adhesive tape to secure one end of the braids to the back of the head.

Now you are ready to style the braids! What color beads do you have? Can you make patterns with them? You could totally add fun clips and cuffs, too!

# BARBERSHOP STYLES

**Wipeable boards are a great way to create fun hairstyles over and over again. Whenever you're ready for a fresh trim, just style, wipe and repeat!**

## Materials Needed

8½ x 11–inch (22 x 28–cm) sheet cardboard or cardstock

Black marker

Scissors

Self-adhesive film

Black dry-erase marker (or any color of your choice)

Cotton swabs

## LET'S CRAFT!

Draw a face with an afro on a piece of cardstock with the black marker. Make the afro quite high so you can create fun styles. Using the scissors, follow the instructions on page 14 to cover the cardstock with self-adhesive film to make it a wipeable board. Now completely color in the afro with a dry-erase marker.

Use the cotton swab to draw and create fun patterns and styles in the hair! Can you see the black color disappear, leaving behind fun lines and patterns? Do you have a favorite sports star or family member with a cool hairstyle? Try using their hair as inspiration!

If you want to change any of your designs, you can color them in again as many times as you want.

## EXTEND YOUR PLAY

*Can you create a mohawk, fades, slick sideburns and cool side parts? What other fun styles can you think of?*

# CHOCOLATE CURLS CUT

Do you love play dough? This curly cutting activity involves homemade chocolate play dough that smells delicious and is fun to squash, squeeze and mold into shapes. And then you can enjoy cutting and playing with it! Cutting play dough is a fun sensory experience. We will make a wipeable board for the perfect reusable play dough mat!

## Materials Needed

1 batch chocolate Play Dough (page 10)

8½ x 11–inch (22 x 28–cm) sheet cardstock or cardboard

Black marker and/or colored pens

Scissors

Self-adhesive film

Play dough tools (rolling pin, potato masher, forks, etc.)

## LET'S CRAFT!

Prepare the chocolate play dough according to the instructions on page 10 and set it aside.

Draw a face on a piece of cardstock using the black marker and/or colored pens, and leave the hair area blank. Using the scissors, follow the instructions on page 14 to cover the cardstock with self-adhesive film to make it a wipeable board.

Cut ten small pieces off the play dough. Roll each piece between the palms of your hands until it is a long sausage shape.

Now twist the play dough sausages into spirals and repeat until you have ten curls. Lay out the play dough curls in the hair area around the face on your wipeable board.

Now enjoy cutting and molding the curls!

## EXTEND YOUR PLAY

*Using your play dough tools, have a go at braiding the play dough. Can you create a bantu knots style? Play dough is so versatile; if you use your imagination, you can make absolutely anything with it!*

# HAIRSTYLE PORTRAITS

This is a great craft to do with a friend. Once you have made your very own wipeable frame, take turns drawing each other!

The wipeable board makes it easy to create new portraits again and again.

## Materials Needed

8½ x 11–inch (22 x 28–cm) sheet cardstock

Black marker

Colored pens

Scissors

Self-adhesive film

Dry erase marker

Mirror (optional)

## LET'S CRAFT!

Draw a frame on a sheet of cardstock with a black marker. Why not make your frame colorful and add patterns with colored pens, too! Leave the center blank. Using the scissors, follow the instructions on page 14 to cover the cardstock with self-adhesive film to make it a wipeable board.

Sit opposite a friend and have a go at drawing them using a dry erase marker. Once you have finished, you can wipe the frame clean and let your friend try drawing you!

You could also try making a self-portrait. Just grab a mirror and try to draw your own face. Don't forget your hair!

## CREATIVE TIP

*Challenge a friend to draw you with a specific hairstyle in specific colors—blue bantu knots or purple curly buns, for example. How about multicolored braids?*

# MIXED-SPICE PLAY DOUGH CURLS

Making your own play dough is so quick and fun, and you can find most of the ingredients in your kitchen cupboards. Check out the mixed-spice Play Dough recipe on page 10 for this project. You'll have fun for hours as you style and decorate your very own play dough locs.

## Materials Needed

1 batch mixed-spice Play Dough (page 10)

8½ x 11–inch (22 x 28–cm) sheet cardstock or cardboard

Black marker

Scissors

Self-adhesive film

Hair styling accessories (gold and silver cuffs, beads, shells, etc.)

Play dough tools (rolling pin, potato masher, forks, etc.)

## LET'S CRAFT!

Prepare the play dough according to the instructions on page 10 and set it aside.

Draw a face with an afro on a piece of cardstock with the black marker. Using the scissors, follow the instructions on page 14 to cover the cardstock with self-adhesive film to make it a wipeable board.

Cut ten small pieces off the play dough. Roll each piece between the palms of your hands until it is a long snake shape.

Lay them out in the hair area around the face on your wipeable board to create "wavy curls."

Now you can add a range of accessories to really make the style pop! Which accessories are your favorite to decorate with?

Enjoy molding, squishing, rolling, flattening and styling the curls!

# STYLING TOOL CARDS

**Do you like to play memory card games? What about puzzles? Well, with these DIY cards, you can play both these games and more!**

## Materials Needed

Scissors

Cardboard or a recycled cereal box

Pencil

Black marker

Colored pens, pencils or markers

## LET'S CRAFT!

Cut six 4½ x 3–inch (11 x 8–cm) cards from the cardboard.

Use the pencil and black marker to draw a different styling tool on each card. For example, I added a satin bonnet, a comb and a bristle brush to some of my cards. What other styling tools can you think of?

Color your drawings in with colored pens once they are complete, then cut each card in half. Now you are ready to play alone or with a partner.

For instance, you and a friend can turn the cards over and play memory. Just take turns picking two cards at a time, and when you get a matching pair, you can keep the cards. Whoever has the most pairs wins.

Can you think of some other games to play with your cards?

## EXTEND YOUR PLAY

*Grab a timer, a few batches of colored rice (see page 12) and a tray. Hide the cards, face down, and cover them with the colored rice. Who can find the matching pairs and put them together correctly the quickest?*

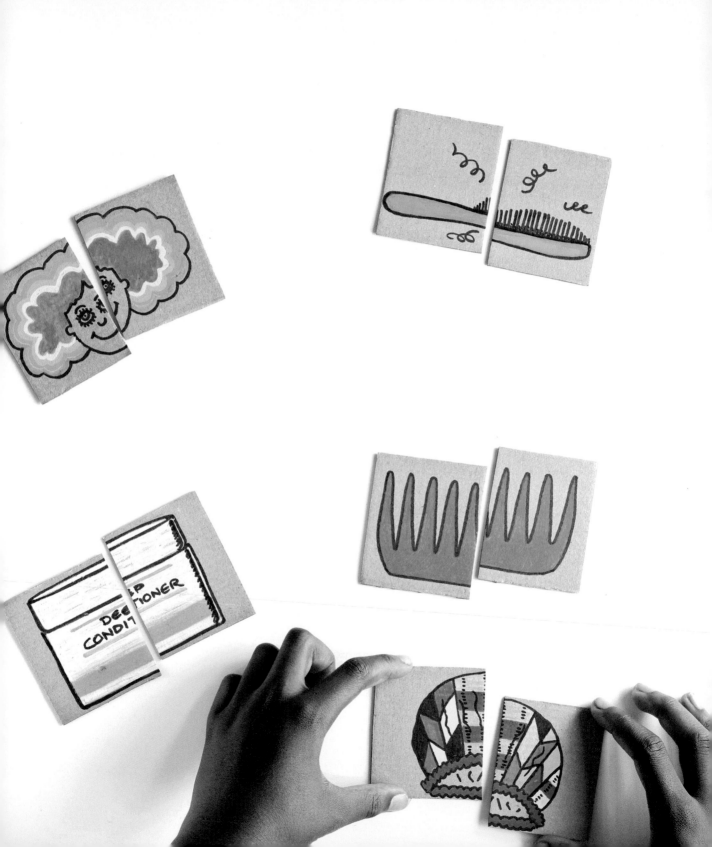

# FABRIC HEAD WRAP ART

You can create an amazing piece of mosaic-style art using any variety of fabrics you have available. You could even use old clothing—but ask a grown-up first!

## Materials Needed

8½ x 11–inch (22 x 28–cm) sheet cardstock or cardboard

Pencil

Black marker

Scissors

Fabrics in a variety of colors and patterns

Plate

Paintbrush

Craft glue

## LET'S CRAFT!

Draw a picture of a woman with a head wrap on a sheet of cardstock with the pencil and black marker. It does not have to be a complicated drawing since you will be covering it all with colorful fabric.

Using scissors, cut up the pieces of fabric into small squares, or circles if you prefer, and put them on a plate. Using a paintbrush, apply glue to each fabric piece and adhere them to different sections of the head wrap until it is all complete.

I love the colors used here. What colored fabric did you use? The more varied the textures of the fabric are the more exciting it will look! There are no rules, so just have fun crafting!

# HEAD WRAP WINDOW ART

**The window art we create always ends up staying on our garden door windows for months. When the sun is shining, the colors reflect onto the ground. It is so pretty!**

## Materials Needed

8½ x 11–inch (22 x 28–cm) sheet cardstock or cardboard

Pencil

Black marker

Scissors

Cellophane in different colors

Glue stick

Sticky tack

## LET'S CRAFT!

Draw a picture of a woman with a head wrap on a sheet of cardstock with the pencil and black marker. Draw the head wrap as simply as possible so that it will be easy to cut out.

Lightly fold the cardstock in different areas of the head wrap. Using scissors, begin to cut out different sections, leaving a border of about 1 inch (2.5 cm). Ask an adult for help if you need it.

Next, cut pieces of cellophane in different colors to fit slightly over the cut-out areas. Now turn the drawing over and glue the cellophane pieces to the cardstock and to each other using the glue stick. Repeat until you have filled all the gaps with cellophane.

Use sticky tack to hang your artwork on a window and enjoy the sun shining through the colorful cellophane.

## CREATIVE TIP

*If you cannot find cellophane at your local craft store or online, you can use cellophane from caramel and hard candy wrappers.*

# Crafty, FLUFFY FUN

Welcome to a chapter of fluffy fun!

It is all about using fuzzy, fluffy, soft materials such as pipe cleaners, pom-poms and wool. Using such materials is a delightful sensory experience that makes crafting fun. You will explore painting with cotton balls (page 98) and threading with pipe cleaners (page 106), in addition to making cool Popsicle stick puppets for playing with friends (page 97) and creating a colorful afro without using any paint or paintbrushes (page 105).

# CURLY BEAD THREADING

Have you crafted with pipe cleaners before? You can bend and mold them into a variety of shapes, and they are perfect for a range of craft activities.

If you are like me and have a drawer full of hair beads, then you are already prepared for this activity! If not, you can use any beads from a local craft shop.

## Materials Needed

8½ x 11–inch (22 x 28–cm) sheet cardstock or cardboard

Black marker and/or colored pens

10–15 pipe cleaners in any colors

Craft glue

Adhesive tape

Beads

## LET'S CRAFT!

Draw a face with a curly afro on a piece of cardstock using the black marker and/or colored pens.

Curl the pipe cleaners by wrapping each one tightly around your finger, then slowly pull your finger out. You should have a tight curl! When you have curled all of the pipe cleaners, glue about ½ inch (1.3 cm) of one end of each pipe cleaner to the hair section of the head. You might want to add a little adhesive tape to secure the pipe cleaners more tightly to the cardstock.

You should have a full head of curls now!

How amazing does your curly person look? Now you can begin to decorate the curls with beads!

What color beads are your favorite? How many can you get on each curl?

## EXTEND YOUR PLAY

*Try plaiting the pipe cleaners to make braids instead.*

# POPSICLE STICK CURLY PUPPETS

Ever wondered what you can do with popsicle sticks? Try creating these curly puppets and putting on a little show with them.

These are so simple to make and fun to play with too!

## Materials Needed

Black marker

Cardboard or recycled cereal box

Scissors

Craft glue

Popsicle sticks (large or regular sized)

Colored felt sheets or construction paper

## LET'S CRAFT!

Using a black marker, draw five circles on a piece of cardboard that are approximately 2 inches (5 cm) in diameter. Draw a face on each of them, cut them out with scissors and glue them each to the end of a popsicle stick. These are your puppets.

For their hair, draw a template of a curly afro on a piece of cardboard and cut it out. Measure it against one of the puppets to ensure the hair doesn't cover the eyes and other features. If it does, cut off more from the template until it is a perfect fit.

Once you are happy with your afro template, trace around it on the pieces of colored felt, making one afro for each puppet. If you want to be a little more creative, you could try to cut out different-sized afros or hairstyles.

Cut the afros out and glue them on the puppets. What do you think? Now have a bit of fun with them!

## CREATIVE TIP

*Try to come up with a little theatre play using your puppets. Can you make up a fun story to show to your friends and family?*

# COTTON BALL CURLS

**Did you know you can paint with cotton balls? That's right! No paintbrushes are needed to create this amazing colorful 'fro!**

## Materials Needed

8½ x 11–inch (22 x 28–cm) sheet cardstock or cardboard

Black marker and/or colored pens

Clothespins

Cotton balls

Paint

## LET'S CRAFT!

Draw a face with a curly afro on a sheet of cardstock using the black marker and/or colored pens, making the hair section as big as possible so you have lots of space to paint. I suggest leaving most of the top half of your paper blank for your painting.

Count out enough clothespins so there is one for each color of paint you're using. Clamp each clothespin onto a cotton ball. You will use these to create colorful curls.

Holding the clothespin, dip the cotton ball in paint so that it covers the tip. Now gently press the painted cotton ball onto the cardstock and twist the clothespin around until you have created a circle. Dip the other cotton balls in the other colors of paint and get creative!

Can you make different-sized circles? I bet your colorful curls are amazing!

# COTTON PAD CURLS

**Don't you just love when colors mix to create beautiful patterns and shades?**

**When you paint on cotton pads, the colors mix and blend so beautifully, and it looks amazingly bright and colorful!**

## Materials Needed

Black marker and/or colored pens

Thin cardboard

Craft glue

Cotton pads

Scissors (optional)

3 or 4 small bowls

Water

Food coloring

Water droppers or pipettes

## LET'S CRAFT!

Using the black marker and/or colored pens, draw a face on a piece of thin cardboard, leaving space for your curls. Using dabs of glue, stick the cotton pads onto the hair area until it's covered.

You might want to cut some of the cotton pads in half like I did so they fit nicely within the 'fro.

Set it aside to dry.

Once the glue is dry, fill the bowls about halfway with water. Add a few drops of food coloring to each one.

Using the droppers, suck up small amounts of the colored water and drop it gently onto the cotton pads. Can you see the colors travel? And what happens when you drop one color onto another? Try it and see!

# POM-POM PUSH

One of our favorite craft decorations is pom-poms, and they are amazing for sensory play too! You can use them to paint or to decorate, but in this project, you'll get to use them to make a fun matching game. I think their versatility is why we love them so much!

## Materials Needed

Scissors

Cardboard

8½ x 11–inch (22 x 28–cm) cardboard box or shoebox

Black marker

Small pom-poms or felt balls

Colored pens

Craft glue

Screwdriver

Sharp pencil

## LET'S CRAFT!

Cut out a square of cardboard that fits well on the cardboard box.

With the black marker, draw a face with curly hair on the cardboard square. Choose your pom-pom colors and find colored pens to match. Now draw simple spirals in each individual color on the afro. Cut out and glue the face to the cardboard box.

Once dry, ask a grown-up to pierce a hole in the center of each spiral with a screwdriver. Each hole must go all the way through both the cardboard face and the cardboard box.

Insert a sharp pencil into each hole and give it a wiggle to make the holes slightly bigger and smoother.

Now you are ready to play! Can you match the pom-poms to the correct color curl? How about a challenge with a friend? Who can push the pom-poms in the holes the quickest? Make sure the colors match though!

# POM-POM 'FRO

**Do you enjoy the feel of fluffy, spongy pom-poms? I do! This crafty afro is fun to make and is so bright and colorful, you might even want to hang it up in your bedroom!**

## Materials Needed

Cardboard or a recycled cereal box

Black marker and/or colored pens

Craft glue

Multicolor pom-poms

## LET'S CRAFT!

Draw a face with an afro on a piece of cardboard with the black marker and/or colored pens. Don't make the afro too large, though, since the pom-poms are small.

Start gluing the pom-poms to the afro. Can you make rainbow patterns of colors, or will you mix all the colors like we have?

Take your time and be as creative as you like!

# PIPE CLEANER CURL DROP

Pipe cleaners make the best curls! They are so easy to twist into large or small spirals. This craft might take a bit of time and patience, but it will be worth it! A glue gun is required, so you will need a grown-up to help you.

## Materials Needed

2 pieces of cardboard

Black marker and/or colored pens

Scissors

Craft knife (ask a grown-up to help with this)

Clear plastic 3-ring binder pouch

Glue stick

Thin cardboard

Glue gun (ask a grown-up to help with this)

Multicolor pipe cleaners

## LET'S CRAFT!

Draw a face with a simple afro shape on a piece of cardboard with the black marker and/or colored pens.

Cut around the whole face and hair. Then, ask an adult to use a craft knife to cut out the inner part of the afro. Be careful not to cut the edges.

Trace the outline of the afro onto the binder pouch and cut it out. You will have two plastic sheets. Glue one of the plastic sheets to the afro.

Now cut a few thin pieces of cardboard into ½-inch (1.3-cm) strips. This will be used to create the gap between the face and the cardboard behind it.

Trace the outline of the complete afro again on the other piece of cardboard. It is important that you leave a gap of 2½ inches (6 cm) at the very top part of the outline.

With an adult's help, follow the instructions on page 11 to turn the afro into a sensory base with the cardboard strips, scissors and glue gun. Don't forget to leave the gap free on the top, as this is where you will be dropping your pipe cleaner curls.

Ask a grown-up to use the glue gun again to adhere your curly picture on top of the border you have just created. Run the glue quickly along the thin strips and place the face you drew on top of the glue so that it sticks well.

Leave this to dry. In the meantime, make your pipe cleaner curls. It's super easy: Just hold on to one end of a pipe cleaner and create flat spirals with both hands, as shown in the picture.

Once you have about fifteen pipe cleaner curls, it's time to drop them into your 'fro!

How amazing does it look with all those spirals of color?

# BOW BALL DROP

**Have you ever made your own ball drop before? It's the perfect activity to repurpose an empty shoebox lid. And it's a great game to play with your friends!**

## Materials Needed

Old shoebox lid or small cardboard box cut to size

Black marker and/or colored pens

Craft knife (ask a grown-up to help with this)

Pom-poms and felt balls

## LET'S CRAFT!

Draw a picture of a face with an afro and hair accessories on the inside of the shoebox lid using the black marker and/or colored pens. Color it in. Choose one or more of the hair accessories and ask an adult to use the craft knife to cut a small hole in the middle of it, just slightly bigger than a pom-pom. I chose the middle of the bow.

Now it is time to have fun!

Starting at the farthest corner of the lid, drop the pom-pom and try to move the lid to get the pom-pom through the hole. The trick is, you can't use your hands to move the pom-pom; you can only move the box lid! To make it more difficult, you can try it with your eyes closed. Also try it with a friend and see how quickly you both can get more than one pom-pom through the hole!

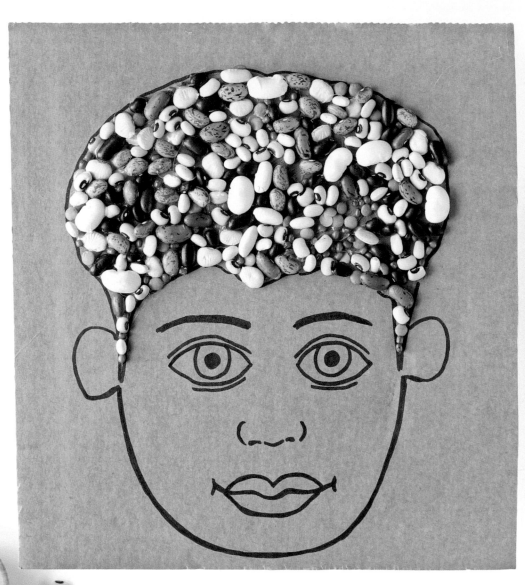

# Creative Crafts
# FROM THE KITCHEN TO THE BACKYARD

Don't you just love to collect nature treasures when you visit the park or the forest? You can use those treasures for fun crafts and art!

Natural materials include flowers and their petals, leaves, stones, sticks, bark, fruits, vegetables and more! Crafting with items from nature is such a fun, sensory experience.

Enjoy painting Cauliflower Curls (page 115) and explore the texture of colored spaghetti pasta with Noodle Faces (page 119).

As you create and craft with these amazing natural materials, appreciate how they smell, look and feel. It is also an opportunity to talk about different colors, shapes and textures.

Another advantage of using natural materials is that they don't cost a thing!

# POPCORN PUFF

**Get ready to create a colorful afro. But this is no ordinary afro. It's a gorgeous curly puff made with yummy popcorn! That's right—if you like popcorn, you will love creating this popcorn art.**

## Materials Needed

1 batch Popcorn (page 9)

Shallow bowl

Black marker and/or colored pens

8½ x 11–inch (22 x 28–cm) sheet cardstock or cardboard

Craft glue

Paints

Paintbrush

## LET'S CRAFT!

Prepare a batch of Popcorn according to the instructions on page 9. Place it in a shallow bowl and set it aside.

Using the black marker and/or colored pens, draw a face on a sheet of cardstock. You can color in the face and features if you choose to.

Think about anyone you know with curly hair. What does their hair look like? Try drawing the biggest afro hair outline that will fit on your page.

Glue the popcorn to the cardstock until it completely fills the space you made for the hair.

Once the glue has dried, it is time to paint the popcorn. What does it feel like when you paint it? Get creative and have fun!

## EXTEND YOUR PLAY

*Try to guess how much popcorn it will take to fill the hair section. Write down your guess and invite other friends and family to do the same before you begin gluing the popcorn.*

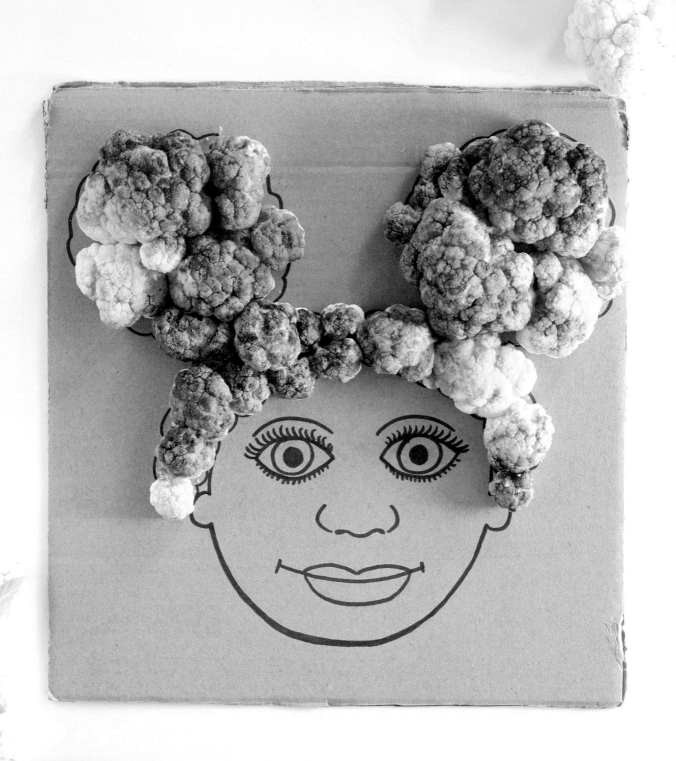

# CAULIFLOWER CURLS

**Have you ever tried painting on vegetables before? It might sound strange, but I know you are going to love it!**

**Whenever you have old vegetables in the fridge, don't throw them away—paint them!**

## Materials Needed

Cauliflower

Kitchen towel

Scissors or knife (ask a grown-up to help with this)

Cardboard

Black marker and/or colored pens

Craft glue or glue gun (ask a grown-up to help with this)

Paints

Paint palette or plate

Paintbrushes

## LET'S CRAFT!

Ask a grown-up to help you prepare the cauliflower. Use a kitchen towel to make sure the vegetables are completely dry. Ask a grown-up to help you remove the stem at the base of the cauliflower with scissors or a knife. Then cut off the individual florets and cut down their stems so each piece has a flat surface.

Set the cauliflower florets aside.

Draw a picture of a face on a piece of cardboard with the black marker and/or colored pens, leaving the hair section free.

Now glue the cauliflower florets to the hair section of the head to create a textured 'fro. Allow it to dry.

Once the glue has dried and the florets are stuck down firmly, prepare your favorite paint colors on a palette or plate.

Now you can paint the "hair"! Dab the paint onto the cauliflower so that you can get the paint into all the crevices.

Use different colors and experiment with making different patterns.

## LET'S TALK

*How does the cauliflower feel? How would you describe the texture of your own hair?*

*You could also try this with broccoli or any other vegetables too!*

# CURLY CELERY PRINTING

**We absolutely love exploring with fruits and vegetables. Did you know that you can turn ordinary fruits and vegetables into stamps and painting tools? Celery in particular makes the most amazing prints!**

## Materials Needed

Celery stalk (expired celery would work well for this craft)

Knife (ask a grown-up to help with this)

Elastic band or string

Cardboard

Black marker and/or colored pens

Paints

Large paint palette or plate

Paintbrush

## LET'S CRAFT!

You will be using the bottom section of a stalk of celery, as well as individual ribs of celery. Ask a grown-up to prepare the celery by cutting about ½ inch (1.3 cm) off the bottom of the stalk using a knife. The cross-section almost looks like a rose, doesn't it?

Secure the ribs of the celery stalk with an elastic band and set it aside.

Draw a face with an afro on a piece of cardboard with a black marker and/or colored pens.

Prepare your paints on a large paint palette or plate. Now it is time to celery paint! Apply a thin layer of paint to the cut end of your celery "rose" with a paintbrush.

Press down hard on the cardboard and lift the celery off gently. How cool is your curl print?

You could get creative and use individual celery ribs to create further curl patterns.

# NOODLE FACES

**Do you love to play and explore with food? It's fun to create shapes and art with food too—especially cooked pasta! Explore making colored spaghetti pasta in this craft and use it to create your own pasta faces and curls!**

## Materials Needed

Cardboard

Black marker and/or colored pens

Scissors

Self-adhesive film

Spaghetti

Water

Large pot

Olive oil or coconut oil

4 resealable plastic bags

Food coloring in 4 different colors

Baking sheet

Parchment paper

## EXTEND YOUR PLAY

*Try making some curly shapes with the spaghetti. Can you draw different hairstyles on a piece of paper and try to copy it with the pasta?*

## LET'S CRAFT!

Draw a face with an outline of an afro on a piece of cardboard with the black marker and/or colored pens. Using the scissors, follow the instructions on page 14 to cover the thin cardboard with self-adhesive film to make it a wipeable board.

Next, it's time to cook the pasta. You will need a grown-up to help you with the stove.

Boil the spaghetti in a large pot of water for about 4 minutes LESS than the time recommended on the package. Don't overcook it! Once cooked, drain the pasta, then put the pasta back into the pot and add cold water to cool it down.

Once cool, drain the pasta again and toss the pasta to coat it in the oil to keep it from sticking. Separate the cooked pasta into four resealable plastic bags. Add a few drops of food coloring to each bag of pasta, seal the bag and shake!

Line a baking sheet with parchment paper. Pour out the colored spaghetti on the tray and leave it to dry for about 30 minutes.

Grab your wipeable board, scissors and colored pasta. It's time to get creating!

Start by adding the facial features and expressions to the face with the pasta. How does it feel in your hands?

Now for the hair! What type of hair will you add? Can you make swirly, whirly, curly hair? Use the scissors to cut smaller pieces and get creating!

# AFRO'CKS (AFRO ROCKS)

Rock painting is one of our favorite activities since my son loves to collect rocks and stones. Have you done rock painting before? You will love creating fun rock people and adding colorful afros!

## Materials Needed

Paint pens

Large rocks or stones

Black marker

Felt-tip pens/chalk pens

Cardboard

## LET'S CRAFT!

Using your paint pens, draw faces with a range of emotions on the rocks you have collected. Be as creative as you want and use as many colors as you wish.

Now use the black marker and pens to draw and decorate a range of afros and hairstyles such as bantu knots, locs or a frohawk on a piece of cardboard.

Now mix and match the face rocks with the afros. How do they look? Pretty cool!

# FLOWERY 'FRO

**Have you ever had a bunch of flowers at home that have started to wilt? Don't throw them out! You can create amazing art with them. Why not try out these flowery curls? Make sure you ask a grown-up before you use their flowers though.**

## Materials Needed

Thin cardboard

Black marker and/or colored pens

Scissors

Cardboard

Cut flowers with the stems removed

Tray

Craft glue

## LET'S CRAFT!

Draw a face with an afro on a piece of thin cardboard with the black marker and/or colored pens.

Using scissors, cut out lots of small squares of cardboard approximately 1 x 1 inch (2.5 x 2.5 cm). You will be gluing the flowers on these first before you add them to the hair section.

Lay out your flowers on a tray, then arrange them on the afro to get an idea of where you will place them.

Once they are in place, pick up one flower at a time and glue it to one of the small cardboard squares, then glue the cardboard square to the hair. Repeat this process until you have a full, blooming 'fro!

## CREATIVE TIP

*Why not try this project using individual flower petals instead? I wonder what amazing art you would create using a range of different colored petals.*

# DAZZLING DREADLOCKS

This is a tricky, sticky activity to strengthen your finger muscles.

You can use a variety of dried beans or legumes if you do not have dried chickpeas—just check your cupboards at home for what you might already have to create this dazzling dreadlock art.

## Materials Needed

Thin cardboard

Black marker and/or colored pens

Dried chickpeas

Bowl

Craft glue

Paints

Glitter

Paint palette

Paintbrush

## LET'S CRAFT!

Draw a face with dreadlocks on a piece of thin cardboard using a black marker and/or colored pens.

Put your dried chickpeas in a bowl so they are easy to grab.

Add a drop of glue to one end of the first dreadlock and stick on one or two chickpeas. Continue this process until all the dreadlocks are filled with chickpeas.

Wait for it to dry.

Mix each paint color with about 1 tablespoon (13 g) of glitter on your paint palette, and then you are ready to turn your chickpea dreadlocks into a dazzling, glittery work of art!

## CREATIVE TIP

*I threw some extra glitter on at the end before the paint dried for some extra sparkle!*

## WHAT DO YOU KNOW ABOUT LOCS?

*Locs are an iconic hairstyle and look great! They are considered a protective style because they do not require any chemicals to create them. The term "locs" or "dreadlocks" is used to describe the style in which hair falls into ropelike strands that form when the hair locks into itself.*

# PINECONE CURLIES

I love when you can make crafts with objects found in nature. If you do not already have a few pinecones around, take a trip to the park or forest and go on a pinecone hunt!

These pinecone people are a lot of fun and gave us the giggles. I know you'll have a lot of fun making them too.

## Materials Needed

Thin cardboard

Black marker and/or colored pens

Felt-tip pens

Scissors

Craft glue

Pinecones

## LET'S CRAFT!

Draw a few small circles on a piece of thin cardboard and draw a face on each one using the black marker and/or colored pens. Your pinecone faces should be about the same size as your pinecones. You can add different expressions and colors if you wish with the felt-tip pens. Cut them out using scissors.

For each face you've made, cut a small strip of thin cardboard, approximately ½ x 2 inches (1.3 x 5 cm), and fold the strip in half.

Glue one side of the strip to the back of each face. The fold should be right near the top of the head and leave the other side of the fold sticking outward.

Once they are all complete and the glue has dried, you can now feed the extended piece of the strip into one of the grooves in the pinecone to create the "hair." Now, how cute are they? Did they make you giggle too?

# FRUITY 'FRO

**This is a fun craft to do, especially if you have some citrus fruits about to expire. The process is so much fun, and it smells amazing!**

## Materials Needed

Various citrus fruits (expired fruits would work well for this craft)

Knife (ask a grown-up to help with this)

Cutting board

Baking sheet

Parchment paper

Black marker and/or colored pens

Cardboard or a recycled cereal box

Paints

Paint palette

Paintbrush

Craft glue

## LET'S CRAFT!

Ask a grown-up to slice the citrus fruits into thin, ⅓-inch (1-cm) slices.

Line a baking sheet with parchment paper and spread the slices out on the tray.

Ask a grown-up to help you bake them on the lowest setting of your oven, approximately 150°F (65°C). Depending on your oven, they might need to bake for up to 5 hours! Turn the slices every hour until the fruit has dried out. Remove them from the oven and let them cool overnight. How beautiful do they look? And doesn't your kitchen smell lovely?

It is time to get your afro art on!

Using the black marker and/or colored pens, draw a face with the outline for your fruity afro on a piece of cardboard.

Choose a couple of dried fruit slices to make prints with. Pour a few drops of paint onto a palette. Using a paintbrush, gently apply paint onto all the now-hard segments to ensure they print clearly. Press the fruit slice quite hard onto the cardboard to create fruity prints. Don't forget to leave some space to glue on some of your fruit slices too!

## CREATIVE TIPS

*The thinner the fruit slices are, the easier they will be to dry. Once they are completely dry, they can be stored for months in an airtight container.*

*Try this project with other fruits such as strawberries or pineapples. Imagine those colors!*

# FAMILY TREE

We love collecting leaves on our walks or trips to the park. What about you? The next time you collect some, you must give this tree craft a go! It involves drawing on leaves, which is a very calming activity.

## Materials Needed

Cardboard or a recycled cereal box

Black marker and/or colored pens

Craft glue

Various sticks

Paint or chalk pens

5 leaves

## LET'S CRAFT!

Spread your fingers wide and place your hand on the cardboard. Use the black marker and/or colored pens to trace around your hand and arm to create a tree trunk and branches.

Glue the sticks to the tree's trunk and set it aside to dry.

With your paint pens, draw one member of your family on each leaf. When you are finished, glue the leaves to the tree.

## LET'S TALK

*When drawing your family and friends, can you describe them? What type of hair do they have? How would you describe their skin color? Can you remember what color eyes they have? What is your favorite thing about the people you're drawing?*

# DRIED BEANS HI-TOP

**These bean and lentil collages look so great and are so much fun to create. It might get a little sticky, but that is all part of the fun!**

## *Materials Needed*

Black marker and/or colored pens

Cardboard or a recycled cereal box

Craft glue

Various dried beans and lentils

## LET'S CRAFT!

With a black marker and/or colored pens, draw the face of a friend or family member on a piece of cardboard, leaving space on the top to draw a hi-top style.

Now you are ready to create amazing patterns on the afro! Glue the beans and lentils on the cardboard and be as creative as you like with filling in the hair area.

# POTATO PRINT FACES

**Have you ever made potato prints before? This is a great craft because the potato prints create perfect face shapes and leave amazing marks and patterns when you lift them off the page.**

## Materials Needed

2 or 3 potatoes in different sizes (expired potatoes would work well with this craft)

Knife (ask a grown-up to help with this)

Paints in skin tone colors (or try creating your own skin tones by mixing red, yellow, white and blue paints)

Plate or paint palette

Paintbrush

Cardboard

Black marker

Felt-tip markers

## LET'S CRAFT!

Gather your potatoes and ask a grown-up to help you cut them in half. These are your potato stamps!

Prepare the paints on a plate or paint palette and dip the cut side of the potatoes in the paint, using a paintbrush to get rid of any excess paint.

Press the potato stamp down hard on the cardboard to create a potato print. This is one of your faces.

Try a variety of different colors or skin tones with other potato stamps until you have a range of faces on the page. Leave it to dry so it will be ready to draw faces on.

Once your face prints are dry, use markers to draw a face and hair on each circle. Try adding different facial expressions, emotions and hairstyles.

Never underestimate what you can do with a potato!

### CREATIVE TIP

*Why not try using an apple half to make apple print faces? Or you could combine potato and apple prints!*

# PASTA 'FRO

There are so many different types and shapes of dried pasta, and they are perfect to play and create with. If you ever find any curly-looking pasta in your kitchen, you should give this craft a try!

## Materials Needed

Cardboard or a recycled cereal box

Black marker and/or colored pens

Dried pasta

Bowl

Craft glue

Paints

Paintbrushes

## LET'S CRAFT!

Draw a face with an afro on a piece of cardboard with the black marker and/or colored pens, and put the dried pasta in a bowl.

Glue the pasta to the hair area of the cardboard until it is filled. Prepare the paints while the glue is drying. You can use one color or a range of different colors.

Paint the pasta and be as creative as you wish. How does it feel painting on pasta?

Doesn't your pasta curls art look amazing?

# NATURAL HAIR

**Half the fun of crafting with natural materials is collecting the items outdoors. Do you enjoy trips to the park or forest and collecting leaves and sticks? If you do, you will love this activity!**

## Materials Needed

Black marker and/or colored pens

Thin cardboard

Craft glue

Nature finds (leaves, twigs, flowers, pinecones, "helicopter" seeds and more)

## LET'S CRAFT!

Using the black marker and/or colored pens, draw a face with a lovely big afro on a piece of thin cardboard.

Glue twigs around the outline of the afro. It might help to break some of them to fit.

Now fill and glue the rest of the 'fro with your other nature finds. How beautiful is your natural hair craft!

# CORK CURLIES

Corks are another great craft material worth collecting (although you can buy some from your local craft store). It is so much fun to create these cork curlies, and you can use them to play too!

## Materials Needed

Pencil

Corks

Cardboard or a recycled cereal box

Scissors

Black marker and/or colored pens

Googly eyes

Craft glue

## LET'S CRAFT!

Use a pencil to trace around the head of the cork on a piece of cardboard and draw an afro around it. Cut this out and use it as a template.

Using your template, trace five or six more afros and cut them out. You could change their shape and size so that they are all slightly different. Color them in with curly patterns using the black marker and/or colored pens. You can use lots of different colors.

Now it is time to decorate the corks.

Try drawing faces on the corks. Are yours silly or serious? You can use googly eyes, or you can draw the eyes with your marker.

Once the pen has dried, use a strong glue to attach the afro onto the top of the cork. Aren't they the cutest little curlies?

Once they are dry, you can have some fun with them! You could even do a little puppet show with your DIY cork curlies.

# RAINBOW LOOPS 'FRO

What is your favorite breakfast cereal? My little ones love toasted oat cereal and still call it "loopy cereal." And you guessed it—it makes a perfect curly craft! It's super easy to color and looks great on crafts!

## Materials Needed

1 batch colored cereal (page 12)

Tray

Cardboard or recycled cereal box

Black marker and/or colored pens

Craft glue

## LET'S CRAFT!

Make the colored cereal loops according to the instructions on page 12. Set them aside on a tray until you are ready to use them.

Draw a face with a 'fro on a piece of cardboard with the black marker and/or colored pens. Glue the colored cereal loops to the hair area. You can create a range of patterns or even try to create a rainbow 'fro like we have done!

## CREATIVE TIP

*You could use other cereals for this craft or even combine different cereals for a range of textures. And just like natural hair, which is made up of a range of textures and curls, your curly hair crafts can be very diverse too!*

# FIZZING 'FRO

**If you enjoy science experiments, then you will love this fizzing 'fro! And I am sure you can find most, if not all, of the ingredients you need in your very own kitchen cupboards. Are you ready for some fizzing fun?**

## Materials Needed

Black marker and/or colored pens

Cardboard or a recycled cereal box

4 toilet paper rolls

Craft glue

Deep tray or container

1 batch Fizzing Powder (page 15)

Food coloring

Liquid droppers or medicine dispensers

Vinegar

## LET'S CRAFT!

Using the black marker and/or colored pens, draw a face with a 'fro on a piece of cardboard that would fit comfortably on the toilet paper rolls. Color the 'fro.

Glue the face onto a toilet paper roll so that it can stand up. Repeat this four times.

Once dry, add your faces to a deep tray.

Add 2 tablespoons (28 g) of the fizzing powder to each toilet paper roll. Add a couple drops of food coloring of a different color to each toilet paper roll for extra colorful fizz.

Using a liquid dropper, drop some vinegar into each toilet paper roll and watch them fizz! How cool is that? Keep adding vinegar for more fizz, and then enjoy playing with the fizzy, colored liquid too!

# ACKNOWLEDGMENTS

There are so many people who have made this book possible, and I would like to say thank you!

First, I would like to thank my children. They are my biggest inspiration and my biggest fans! They are my craft partners, my mess makers, and I look forward to many years of being creative with them.

My husband, who has supported me and accepted that he now lives in a house full of cardboard crafts! Thank you for chilling with me while I craft in the evenings.

My mum, who has supported me from the very start and always cheered me on!

Thank you to all my family and friends who came together to help me in every way possible! I couldn't have done this without them. I'm so grateful for the help that was extended to me.

To Christian, who spent tireless hours with me and the children taking amazing photographs and being as much a perfectionist as I.

To Page Street, who took a chance on me. Thank you for helping me achieve this book!

And last, to my lovely community of cardboard hoarders and sensory play lovers on Instagram.